SUDAN

...in Pictures

Visual Geography Series®

SUDAN

...in Pictures

Prepared by
Geography Department

Lerner Publications Company
Minneapolis

Two members of the Dinka people of southern Sudan
pass each other on a village road.

This book is an all-new edition in the Visual Geography Series. Previous editions were published by
Sterling Publishing Company, New York City. The
text, set in 10/12 Century Textbook, is fully revised
and updated, and new photographs, maps, charts, and
captions have been added.

LIBRARY OF CONGRESS CATALOGING-IN-PUBLICATION DATA

Sudan in pictures / prepared by Geography Department,
  Lerner Publications Company.

    p. cm. — (Visual geography series)
    Rev. ed. of: The Sudan in pictures / by Salah Khogali
  Ismail. c1976.
    Includes index.
    Summary: Introduces the land, history, government,
  people, and economy of the largest African country
  in area.
    ISBN 0-8225-1839-2 (lib. bdg.)
    1. Sudan. [1. Sudan.] I. Ismail, Salah Khogali. Su-
  dan in pictures. II. Lerner Publications Company.
  Geography Dept. III. Series: Visual geography
  series (Minneapolis, Minn.)
  DT154.6.A24 1988   87–27037
  962.4—dc19   CIP
                                                   AC

International Standard Book Number: 0–8225–1839–2
Library of Congress Catalog Card Number: 87–27037

VISUAL GEOGRAPHY SERIES®

Publisher
Harry Jonas Lerner
Associate Publisher
Nancy M. Campbell
Senior Editor
Mary M. Rodgers
Editor
Gretchen Bratvold
Illustrations Editor
Karen A. Sirvaitis
Consultants/Contributors
Daniel Abebe
Sandra K. Davis
Designer
Jim Simondet
Cartographer
Carol F. Barrett
Indexer
Sylvia Timian
Production Manager
Gary J. Hansen

Independent Picture Service

Cattle gather at a water hole in eastern Sudan.

Acknowledgments

Title page photo courtesy of Kay Chernush/Agency
for International Development.

Elevation contours adapted from *The Times Atlas of
the World*, seventh comprehensive edition (New York:
Times Books, 1985).

2 3 4 5 6 7 8 9 10 97 96 95 94 93 92 91 90

A village outside Kassala in northeastern Sudan is built close to smooth but irregularly shaped rock formations.

Contents

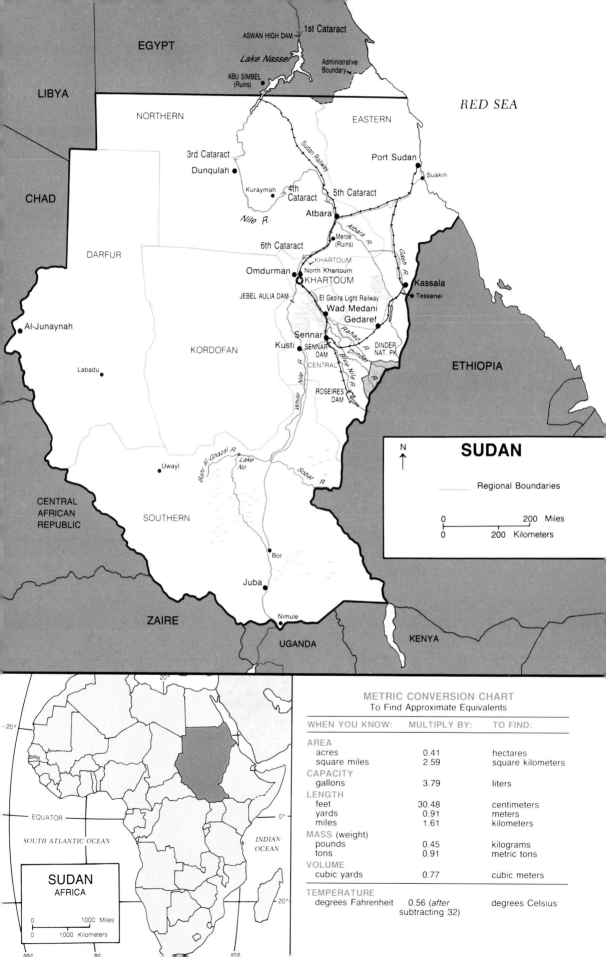

EGYPT

LIBYA

CHAD

1st Cataract

ASWAN HIGH DAM

Lake Nasser

ABU SIMBEL
(Ruins)

NORTHERN

EASTERN

RED SEA

Administrative
Boundary

3rd Cataract

Dunqulah

Kuraymah

4th
Cataract

5th Cataract

Port Sudan

Suakin

Sudan Railway

Nile R.

Atbara

Meroë
(Ruins)

Atbara R.

Gash R.

DARFUR

6th Cataract

KHARTOUM

North Khartoum

KHARTOUM

Omdurman

Kassala

Tessenei

Al-Junaynah

JEBEL AULIA DAM

El Gezira Light Railway

Wad Medani

Gedaref

Labadu

KORDOFAN

Kusti

Sennar

SENNAR
DAM

CENTRAL

DINDER
NAT. PK.

ETHIOPIA

Rahad R.

Blue Nile R.

Dinder R.

ROSEIRES
DAM

White Nile R.

Bahr al-Ghazal R.

Lake
No

Sobat R.

Uwayl

N

SUDAN

Regional Boundaries

0   200 Miles

0   200 Kilometers

CENTRAL
AFRICAN
REPUBLIC

SOUTHERN

Bor

Juba

Nimule

ZAIRE

UGANDA

KENYA

20°

20°

20°

EQUATOR

0°

SOUTH ATLANTIC OCEAN

INDIAN
OCEAN

20°

SUDAN
AFRICA

0   1000 Miles

0   1000 Kilometers

METRIC CONVERSION CHART
To Find Approximate Equivalents

WHEN YOU KNOW:	MULTIPLY BY:	TO FIND:
AREA		
acres	0.41	hectares
square miles	2.59	square kilometers
CAPACITY		
gallons	3.79	liters
LENGTH		
feet	30.48	centimeters
yards	0.91	meters
miles	1.61	kilometers
MASS (weight)		
pounds	0.45	kilograms
tons	0.91	metric tons
VOLUME		
cubic yards	0.77	cubic meters
TEMPERATURE		
degrees Fahrenheit	0.56 (*after* subtracting 32)	degrees Celsius

A man and his donkey cart leave a settlement made up of one-story dwellings packed tightly together in the desert.

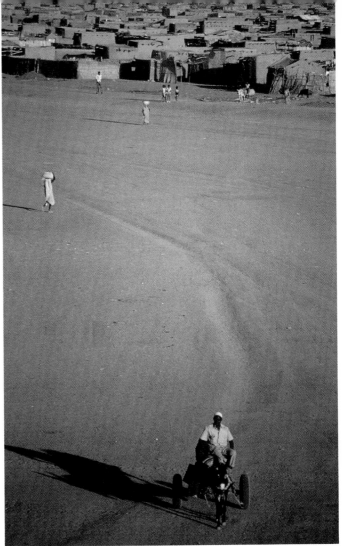

Introduction

An Arab proverb maintains that Allah (the name for God in the Islamic religion) wept when he created Sudan. Another version of the proverb insists Allah laughed on the same occasion. In Sudan the combination of two cultures—Arab and African—has not blended into a peaceful whole. In fact, the mix has been violent, and civil wars and threats of civil wars continue to plague the country.

The largest nation in area on the African continent, Sudan includes vast stretches of desert in the north as well as tropical forests in the south. Grasslands and swamplands exist between the two regions. The peoples of the north see themselves as part of the larger Arab world. The inhabitants of the southern third of the country are linked by their social and cultural heritage to black Africa.

The Muslim north contrasts with the south, where Christianity and local religions prevail. The urbanized and market-based economies of the north differ sharply from the pastoral, agricultural economies of the south. The Muslim-educated, Arabic-speaking elite in northern Sudan has little regard for the Christian-educated, English-speaking southern leadership that developed when Sudan was under British rule.

In 1952, when the British agreed to formulate plans for independence in Sudan, they followed their customary practice of gradually turning over control of the government to a privileged minority. The group the British chose were northerners who had virtually no ties with the peoples of the south. In fact the Umma party was such a minority that few people —even in the north—supported it. An opposition party sponsored the legislation that achieved Sudan's independence in 1956.

When the British left the country, Sudan sank into bitter political and re-

This woman and her child are of the Lotuko people, who live in the war-torn southern region of Sudan.

gional conflicts. By the 1960s, civil war in the south was consuming as much as 30 percent of the national budget.

Once the home of some of the wealthiest ancient kingdoms in the world, Sudan is now one of Africa's poorest and least economically developed nations. No one knows whether the diverse—and often divided—ethnic, religious, and cultural threads of this troubled country can ever be woven together to create a single national identity.

Although the larger portion of Sudan's Christians live in the south, this Roman Catholic church is located in Khartoum to serve Catholics of the capital city.

Northern ethnic groups include the Nubians, two of whom perform a Sudanese folk song using tambourines.

Sudan's sparsely vegetated and generally flat topography is clearly visible in this aerial view.

1) The Land

Sudan occupies about 967,000 square miles in northeastern Africa. It is one-third as large as the mainland United States. Sudan is bordered on the north by Egypt and by a small part of Libya, on the east by the Red Sea and Ethiopia, on the south by Uganda, Kenya, and Zaire, and on the west by Chad and the Central African Republic.

Much of the country's vast area cannot support human life. But large regions maintain sizable populations and produce abundant crops because of the bounty of the Nile River system. The Nile and its network of tributaries, especially the White Nile and the Blue Nile, are vital to the life of Sudan.

Topography

Sudan's territory may be divided into three generally flat regions: deserts in the north; semi-arid plains in the middle; and swampy, tropical forests in the south. Highlands and low mountain ranges rise at the western, eastern, and southern borders.

Sudan's northernmost section is dominated by the Libyan and Nubian deserts, through which the Nile River cuts its route. Also in this region is the southern third of Lake Nasser, which was formed when Egypt built the Aswan High Dam in the 1960s. Sand dunes characterize parts of the landscape, but gravel plains also appear. Oases—fertile, watered areas in the desert that support people, livestock, and vegetation—prevent the far north from being completely unpopulated. Settled populations also have gathered along the banks of the Nile in the Nubian Desert.

East of the desert, an elevated tract of land known as the Red Sea Hills rises to peaks of up to 7,000 feet above sea level. These hills have well-watered valleys that support scrub vegetation in the north and dense growth near the Ethiopian border.

Most of the central part of the country, lying west of the White Nile, consists of high, rolling, sandy plains. At the western end of the plains are the Jebel Marra Mountains of Darfur province. At their eastern end, the plains rise to form the

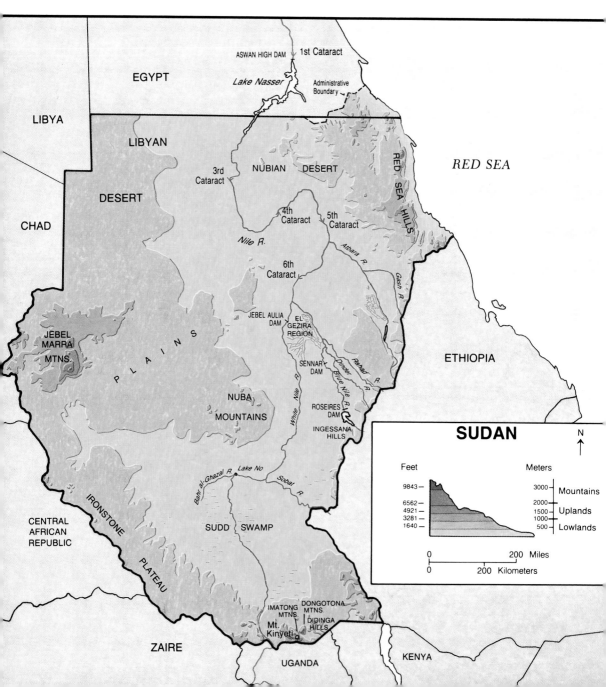

The mountain ranges in Sudan cluster at the nation's southern, eastern, and western borders and extend into neighboring countries.

Nuba Mountains, a region of gray and red granite ridges. East of the White Nile is the fertile El Gezira region that is bounded on the east by the Blue Nile. The easternmost part of this central belt—which stretches southward from Kassala on the Ethiopian border into the provinces of Bahr al-Ghazal and Equatoria—consists of plains of clay soil that are covered with grass.

Sudan's southern region ranges from grasslands to thick forests along the nation's border with Uganda and Zaire. The main features of the lower third of Sudan's territory are a basin drained by the Nile River, the ironstone plateau, and the mountains on the southern border.

The basin experiences the annual flooding of the Nile River and is largely composed of swampland. The ironstone plateau, located along the southwestern border, receives plenty of rain and has a long wet season, which supports an abundance of trees and grasses. Sudan's southern ranges—the Imatong Mountains, the Dongotona Mountains, and the Didinga Hills—border Uganda. Within the Imatong range lies Mount Kinyeti, which, at 10,456 feet, is the highest peak in Sudan.

A Sudanese worker picks cotton in the El Gezira region, where the government operates a large plantation.

Among the reeds of the Blue Nile River near Wad Medani, a Sudanese fisherman adds to his catch of fish.

The Nile River

The rivers of many countries—Tanzania, Kenya, Zaire, Uganda, and Ethiopia—contribute to the waters of the Nile, the longest waterway in the world. Of the river's total volume, 84 percent comes from Ethiopia via the Blue Nile, and 16 percent arrives from Central Africa by way of the White Nile. The entire Nile River Basin covers 1.1 million square miles, an area that is equivalent to about one-tenth of the African continent.

Near its beginning in eastern Africa, the White Nile has various regional names. The most remote source rises in Tanzania about 4,200 miles south of the Mediterranean Sea and flows into Lake Victoria. The White Nile enters Sudan at Nimule, about 3,100 miles from the Mediterranean Sea.

Rapids churn through the next 100 miles of the river's route, after which the waterway spills onto the great plain of Sudan.

Courtesy of Carl Purcell, Eliot Elisofon Archives, National Museum of African Art, Smithsonian Institution

The Nile River receives much of its water volume from the Blue Nile, which snakes through the highlands of Ethiopia before crossing into Sudan.

Courtesy of Kay Chernush/Agency for International Development

Many small rivers join the Nile as it makes its 3,500-mile-long journey from Central Africa north to the Mediterranean Sea. This section of the river cuts through the plains of Sudan.

13

An aerial view of Khartoum shows its geometric layout. The capital is actually reckoned to be three towns – Omdurman, a national capital; Khartoum, the center for commerce and government administration; and North Khartoum, the industrial hub. The three cities are connected by bridges that cross the Blue Nile and the White Nile, which meet on the site.

After winding through a 400-mile swamp, called the Sudd, the river reaches Lake No, where it is joined from the west by the Bahr al-Ghazal River. From this point onward, the waterway is named the White Nile, and its total length from Lake No to the Sudanese capital of Khartoum is about 600 miles. After roughly 80 miles, the Sobat River, which rises in the mountains of Ethiopia, joins the White Nile.

The Blue Nile begins in Lake Tana, which lies on Ethiopia's Amhara Plateau. Its course in Sudan is nearly 500 miles long, and it is joined by the Dinder and Rahad rivers between the cities of Sennar and Khartoum. Unlike the White Nile, which is a sluggish waterway that changes little in appearance from season to season, the Blue Nile is forceful and highly variable.

The main course of the Nile forms at Khartoum, where the White and Blue Nile meet. For the 1,900-mile course from Khar-

toum to the Mediterranean, no constant streams flow into the Nile. The small waterways that do feed the river are dry for much of the year. The Atbara, which joins the main Nile 200 miles north of Khartoum, carries large volumes of water in the flood period, but it is dry for more than half the year. Along the river's course in Sudan, many cataracts (steep rapids or waterfalls) form promising sites for the large-scale development of hydroelectric power.

Flooding

The flooding of the Nile River from seasonal rains is a vital factor in the life of Sudan. Two seasons—the flood period and the rest period—exist. The volume of water in the main Nile at the peak of the flood period (late August and early September) is usually about 16 times that of its lowest stage, which occurs in April.

Surpluses of water occur from mid-July to December, when large volumes pass to the sea.

The rest of the year, from January to mid-July, is the period of shortage, when the Nile does not provide enough water for irrigation. Flood water, however, is called "untimely," because some of it is wasted, while water in the period of shortage is called "timely," because all of it is used.

During the flood period, the Blue Nile discharges 60 times more water than the river contributes during the time of shortage. Normally, rain on the Amhara Plateau affects Sudan by about the middle of May, when the Blue Nile starts to rise. Red silt from flooded lands appears in the river at Khartoum near the end of June. The river rises irregularly until it reaches peak level at Khartoum about the end of August. Later in September, it begins to fall rapidly.

Compared to the Blue Nile, the White Nile is much more steady. The discharge during the flood period is about three times that of the low season. About half the water of the White Nile comes from the Sobat River, which usually starts to rise toward the end of April.

Even more erratic than the Blue Nile, the Atbara River pours down from the northern part of the Amhara Plateau. The waterway starts to rise toward the end of May and joins the Nile in early June. By the end of August the Atbara has fallen rapidly and has dried into a chain of pools.

Rainfall and Climate

The climate of Sudan corresponds roughly to its three main areas—the deserts, the central plains, and the tropical south. Rain in the deserts is rare, and dust storms are common. The central areas have a variable

During the flood period, red topsoil— which is picked up as the river rushes through flooded lands—begins to appear in the Nile.

15

rainy season, and they receive as much as 30 inches of rainfall each year. This area grows much of Sudan's food. On the coast of the Red Sea, precipitation falls mainly in winter, with a secondary rainy season in summer. Southern regions receive the largest amounts of moisture, in some places averaging 55 inches annually.

Supplies of underground water depend on amounts of rainfall, on the shape of the landscape, and on the type of soil in a particular region. In the central clay plain, for example, the clay forms a seal when it is wet, and little or no water sinks beyond the roots of plants. Most of the rainfall, therefore, evaporates into the atmosphere, even in areas that have over 20 inches of precipitation. The White Nile flows over this clay from Bor to Khartoum, losing very little water during the journey.

Differences in elevation determine Sudan's year-round temperatures, which are generally high. The north has temperatures ranging from the upper seventies to over 100° F. Occasionally, the thermometer may reach a mark of 118° F. The central and southern belts benefit from rain and clouds that decrease temperatures in these regions by a few degrees.

Flora and Fauna

In the desert areas of the north and west, vegetation grows only around a few oases. In areas that receive a little rainfall, however, thorny scrub appears, consisting mainly of acacia trees. Various types of grasses sprout during periods of rain, but these wither away quickly after the rains end.

In some parts of central Sudan, small, thorny trees appear from among more permanent grass and other low plants as the rainfall increases. South of this zone, the true savanna (grassland) begins, forming areas of permanent grass with a scattering of trees. Baobab trees, which conserve water in their giant trunks, are a fairly common sight.

In the 1980s, drought occurred in northeastern Sudan. Here, Beja nomads who live in a refugee camp near the Red Sea Hills collect water from a pump.

Gazelles—spindly limbed but swift members of the antelope family—graze on savanna grasses in Dinder National Park located about 300 miles southeast of Khartoum.

16

Baobabs are part of the silk-cotton tree family, and, although they do not grow very tall, their trunks can reach widths of 30 feet in diameter.

Camels continue to provide reliable transport and portage in dry and semi-arid regions of Sudan.

The south contains many forests, but in the Sudd Swamp, the most common plant is papyrus—a tall marsh grass from which the ancient Egyptians made paper. In the forests, typical trees are the giant mahogany, the tamarind, and the sausage tree—so called because of the sausagelike appearance of its edible fruit.

North of the borders of Kenya, Uganda, and Zaire lies an area where some animals still graze and breed. The terrain ranges from thick forest to open, parklike country, where acacias, scrub vegetation, treeless swamps, and high mountains provide a variety of animal habitats.

Buffalo, elephants, rhinoceroses, lions, giraffes, and many varieties of antelope—including giant eland, bongos, and yellow-backed duikers—live in the south. Wild sheep still roam in northern Darfur province, and ibex (wild goats) continue to thrive in the Red Sea Hills.

Workers inspect a steamer that is ready to be overhauled at the dockyards of North Khartoum.

Courtesy of Kenneth J. Perkins
The owners of two dhows—Arab boats of ancient design—relax on the banks of the Nile near Khartoum.

Khartoum

Near the junction of the Blue Nile and the White Nile lies Khartoum (population 1.1 million), the capital city of Sudan. Khartoum province includes the city, the neighboring communities of Omdurman and North Khartoum, and a stretch of the surrounding countryside. Omdurman lies on the White Nile about four miles northwest of Khartoum, while North Khartoum lies directly opposite Khartoum on the other bank of the Blue Nile. The three zones have a combined population that is estimated to be approaching two million people.

In Arabic, Khartoum means "elephant trunk" and was so named because an early resident imagined that the area resembled the long snout of an elephant. The city is handsome and spacious, with a tree-lined walkway along the river and many fine buildings and attractive gardens. The temperature in Khartoum averages 60° F in January and rises to 107° F in May and June. In December, January, and February, no rain occurs, and the summer months bring only a few inches of precipitation.

After war destroyed it in 1885, downtown Khartoum was rebuilt as a modern and spacious city. Colonial-style buildings, from the era when the British controlled Sudan, blend with more traditional structures that are surrounded by trees and shrubbery.

Khartoum is the largest city in Sudan and is growing daily. Drought, economic problems, and unemployment have brought throngs of rural Sudanese to the capital in search of work. Citizens of Khartoum must often wait in long lines to buy the most basic foods.

Secondary Cities

With a metropolitan population of about one million people, Kassala is the largest market town in the agriculturally rich eastern provinces of the country. The Gash River supplies the city with water for irrigation and other purposes. A railway

Independent Picture Service

Kassala, a large trading center in eastern Sudan, is known for its camel and cattle market. Surrounding the city are jagged hills that are an important source of limestone.

A suq, or market, in Omdurman displays a wide variety of handicrafts—including stacks of leather pouches that are made from local materials.

branch leads from Kassala to Tessenei on the Ethiopian frontier, while roads go east into Eritrea, south to Gedaref, and west to Khartoum.

Lying on the coast of the Red Sea, Port Sudan has a population of 206,000. Its excellent port and modern docking facilities make it a major commercial and shipping point. Indeed, most of Sudan's trade with other countries flows through the city's docks.

With a population of more than 120,000, Atbara is the most important city in the northern provinces of Sudan. The headquarters of the Sudan Railway are located in the city, and Sudan's first trade union was established in Atbara.

Wad Medani (population 107,000) is the center of the El Gezira district where the government operates a vast agricultural project. The city's residents were some of the earliest Sudanese to start the movement against British rule. Wad Medani hosted the first congress at which the Sudanese called for self-rule and independence.

An old market town, Gedaref (population 60,000) has grown because of its location in a wide valley. The bowl-shaped landscape helps to collect a water supply that is sufficient for agriculture. Gedaref is the largest market in the country for dura, or Indian millet (a type of grain), which is grown on a large scale in the district.

The well-lit thoroughfares of Khartoum are known for their heavy traffic.

Wad Medani lies along the banks of the Blue Nile River, where herders let livestock wander while they go to the city's market.

Sudan's main harbor is located at Port Sudan along the Red Sea. Built by the British in the early twentieth century, the city is a thriving commercial center, the end point for railway travel in the Nile region, and a shipping hub for Sudanese peanuts, cotton, and oilseeds.

Northern Sudan's early history is strongly linked to the 2,000-year period of the Pharaohs in Egypt. These four huge statues, or colossi, depict Pharaoh Ramses II and are at Abu Simbel, located only 25 miles north of the present Sudanese-Egyptian border. Between 1300 and 1233 B.C., when Ramses II ordered the colossi to be built, the Sudanese kingdom of Cush was under his control.

2) History and Government

Because Sudan's northerners and southerners think of themselves as separate groups, the nation's early history developed in two distinct ways. The northern and central sections of the nation had close ties with developments in Egypt, while the southern region led a more isolated existence. Geographically connected to equatorial Africa, southern Sudan remained relatively undisturbed until the nineteenth century, when Europeans united the two regions into one political unit.

Early History

Ancient Egyptian written records refer to the area now called Sudan. These sources talk about the Cush region, which was located in northern Sudan, near the Nile River system. Trade links between Cush and the Egyptian Empire developed in about 2000 B.C. because Egypt sought gold from the region and captured Cushitic people to use as slaves.

The ups and downs of Egyptian politics —when Pharaohs (rulers or kings) governed the region—touched Cush in various ways. When the Pharaohs were under siege in their own realm, Cush suffered less interference from Egypt. On the other hand, powerful Egyptian rulers sometimes brought Cush within their control.

By the eighth century B.C., Cush had emerged as an independent kingdom centered in Napata, near the fourth cataract (set of rapids) of the Nile. The Egyptians attempted to subdue Napata in 590 B.C. and forced the kingdom to move its capital south to Meroë, near the river's sixth cataract. Although Napata remained the religious focus of the kingdom—several temples still stand there—Meroë functioned as the realm's administrative center. In A.D. 350 an army from the aggressive Aksumite kingdom of northern Ethiopia traveled west and destroyed Meroë, effectively ending the Meroitic kingdom's independent existence.

The Nubian Kingdoms

With the decline of Meroë, smaller realms —Nobatia, Muqurra, and Alwash—took over the Nubian Desert area of northern Sudan. For several centuries these kingdoms resisted domination by the Roman Empire, which was adding territory to its holdings. Friction between the Romans and the early Sudanese was frequent until the Roman emperor Justinian I established Roman influence peacefully—by sending Christian missionaries to Sudan. The first Christian missionary from Constantinople, then the capital of the Roman Empire, reached Nobatia in A.D. 543.

The Nubians gradually adopted the same form of Christianity practiced in Egypt and Ethiopia. The people of the eastern desert and the Red Sea Hills, however, continued to practice their local religions. Ties with Christianity and Egypt brought the Nubian kingdoms into greater contact with Christian cultures that lived around the Mediterranean Sea.

Arab armies threatened the security of the Christian Nubian kingdoms in the seventh century. These forces—whose members followed the faith of Islam and were called Muslims—conquered Egypt. For their own safety, Nobatia and Muqurra joined together to form the kingdom of Dunqulah in about A.D. 700.

Arab Influences

In the seventh century Arab armies entered Nubia and brought Islam with them. But Islam took hold very slowly in northern Sudan, where Christian Nubians still existed in large numbers. Instead of converting the Christian Nubians, the Arabs decided to capture and sell them into slavery as domestic servants or soldiers.

Pyramidlike structures, including the ruins of temples and palaces, are the remains of Meroë, the capital of the Meroitic kingdom until A.D. 350.

Eventually, the religion of Islam took hold in Sudan, and mosques (Islamic houses of worship) were built as meeting places for the growing Muslim community. Faithful Muslims, who are answering the age-old call to prayer, stand outside this mosque in Khartoum.

The Nubians, however, strongly resisted the armies and the new religion. Rather than fight a prolonged war, the Arabs arranged a series of treaties, or *faqt,* with the Nubian kingdoms. Under the treaties, the Nubians promised an annual quota of slaves in exchange for Egyptian goods and produce. The faqt governed relations between the Nubians and the Arabs for 600 years. But the Nubians continued to resist the Arab armies, merchants, and religious leaders that streamed into the area.

Eventually, the Nubian kingdoms faltered as Islamic strength increased. An Islamic class of soldiers called the Mamluks—who were allied with the Turkish Ottoman Empire and who controlled Egypt—conquered Dunqulah in the fourteenth century. The kingdom of Alwash collapsed in 1504, when the Funj sultans established the first Muslim monarchy in Sudan, with its capital at Sennar. The Nubian form of Christianity, having lost contact with other Christian cultures, began

In spite of the Islamic presence, a form of Christianity—called Coptic—survived in Sudan. As a result, early Sudanese Christian artworks show strong Coptic influences.

to wither away and disappeared by the seventeenth century.

The Sultanate of Sennar

The Funj was a loose collection of small realms that recognized the sultan of Sennar as their leader. The capital city was at the center of several trade routes in the region, which the sultanate (kingdom) protected for over three centuries. In exchange for safe caravan routes, the small dependent states contributed taxes and troops on a regular basis.

At the height of its power in the middle of the seventeenth century, the Sennar sultanate repelled attacks by non-Muslim African peoples from the south, by Ethiopian groups to the east, and by Arabs from the north. Because of its military success, the sultanate attempted to centralize its power in the seventeenth and eighteenth centuries. This move meant that the small vassal states would have less influence in the decisions that affected them. The

The city of Suakin, located on the Red Sea south of Port Sudan, was a trade hub for the caravan routes that were protected by the forces of the Sennar sultanate. The city's ruined buildings contrast with an earlier time, when the thriving port traded heavily in gold and slaves.

Under the Turkiya (a period of Turco-Egyptian control), slave raiders captured many Sudanese. The raiders took their captives to protected encampments, such as this one in Kordofan province, before selling them into bondage.

resistance of the vassal states to centralization weakened the sultanate. By the early nineteenth century, the smaller realms had substantially loosened their ties to the sultanate of Sennar.

The Turkiya

In 1811 Muhammad Ali Pasha—a high-ranking official of the Turkish Ottoman Empire in Egypt—conquered the declining sultanate of Sennar. He seized gold and enslaved soldiers for his regime. A second Egyptian army arrived in 1820 and firmly established Egyptian rule—called the Turkiya—in Sudan. In the decades that followed, the Egyptians greatly extended the boundaries of their new territory.

The early period of Turco-Egyptian rule proved harsh for the Sudanese. Officers

The Egyptian army of the Turkish Ottoman Empire established several defensive sites, including this fortress at Suakin.

of the occupying army demanded huge sums of money from the people who lived there, and the soldiers fed themselves from the food that people grew for their families.

The slave trade resumed in order to restock the Egyptian army. Raiders traveled throughout the north, and fleeing populations left their fields untended. In search of slave recruits, hunters went into the southern reaches of Sudan, making contact for the first time with black African ethnic groups. Corruption and the slave trade created widespread unrest among the Sudanese under the Turkiya.

The Mahdi

In the 1880s, Muhammad Ahmad ibn al-Sayyid abd Allah, the son of a boat builder from Dunqulah, began to preach a doctrine of purified Islam. He encouraged the Sudanese to drive the Turks from Sudan. Calling himself *al-Mahdi al-Muntazar* (the Awaited Guide in the Right Path), Muhammad Ahmad was joined by an important Arab religious leader named Abdullahi ibn Muhammad.

Muhammad Ahmad's popularity and Abdullahi's acceptance of him encouraged many people in the countryside to view Muhammad Ahmad as the Mahdi. When the government in Khartoum sought to arrest him, the Mahdi fled with his supporters to Kordofan province. Early in 1882, the Mahdi and his followers, by then 30,000 strong, began an armed resistance against the Egyptian occupying forces. In the following year, the Mahdi's forces gradually gained control over much of northern Sudan.

Meanwhile, Great Britain—a strong world power at the time—had taken control of Egypt in 1882 to protect vital trade routes in the region. When the Mahdi's movement looked successful, the British sent General Charles Gordon to Khartoum in February 1884 with instructions to withdraw the Egyptian troops from Sudan.

Muhammad Ahmad ibn al-Sayyid abd Allah declared himself to be the Mahdi, or Islam's awaited guide, in 1881. He encouraged an Islamic doctrine that aimed to overthrow the Turco-Egyptian troops, and, through his personal popularity, gathered together a well-trained army of followers who were called variously Mahdists, ansar (helpers), and dervishes.

Acting against his government's orders, Gordon maintained the Egyptian forces at Khartoum and believed he could eliminate the Mahdists. In response, the Mahdists attacked Khartoum. Public outcry in Britain to rescue Gordon pressured the British government into sending a relief force. The relief expedition arrived in Khartoum on January 28, 1885. But the Mahdi's forces had already won, and Gordon had died in the fighting. Six months later, the Mahdi died of typhoid fever.

After some internal fighting, a khalifa, or successor to the Mahdi, was chosen. Abdullahi, the Mahdi's first supporter, emerged as the khalifa, and his reign was known as the Mahdiya. Abdullahi had many challenges to face, since several European countries—including Germany,

After the Mahdi's death in 1885, his tomb *(above)* became a pilgrimage site until 1898. In that year the Battle of Omdurman ended Mahdist rule in Sudan. British soldiers *(below)* watch over the slain bodies of the Mahdist leaders, including the Khalifa Abdullahi *(foreground).*

Italy, France, Belgium, and Britain—wanted to claim territory in Africa for their colonial empires.

The Anglo-Egyptian Condominium

The scramble for African colonies made the British troops in Egypt hasten their occupation of Sudan in order to outpace the French. By 1899, after Britain's General Horatio Herbert Kitchener had defeated the Mahdists at Omdurman, a large chunk of land—called Anglo-Egyptian Sudan—was under Anglo-Egyptian control. The Condominium Agreement of 1899 established the joint authority of Britain and Egypt over Sudan. Supreme power was placed in a British governor-general.

Under the condominium, British officers had far-reaching powers. All executive authority—in the form of a council headed by the governor-general—was in the hands of the British. In addition, judicial decisions began to be made within a framework of British laws. Sharia courts—religious tribunals run by Islamic leaders—were allowed, but their decisions could not conflict with the British code.

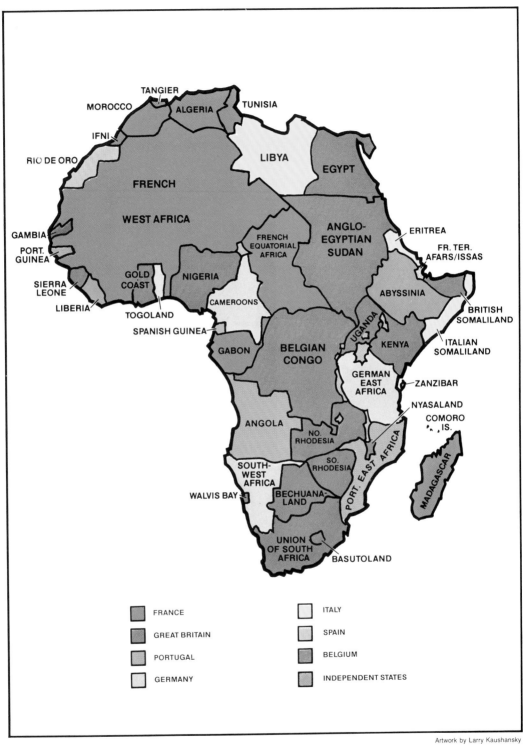

■	FRANCE	□	ITALY
■	GREAT BRITAIN	■	SPAIN
□	PORTUGAL	■	BELGIUM
□	GERMANY	■	INDEPENDENT STATES

Artwork by Larry Kaushansky

After the Battle of Omdurman in 1898, Britain was able to absorb a large chunk of land in northeastern Africa. The colonial power called the new acquisition Anglo-Egyptian Sudan, because both England and Egypt controlled the region. (Map information from *The Anchor Atlas of World History,* 1978.)

Among the developments that occurred under the Condominium Agreement was the laying of rail lines to connect the cities of the north.

Disagreements among ethnic groups occurred, but neither Arabs nor Africans in Sudan organized resistance to the condominium. Government projects developed smoothly in north and central Sudan. Telegraph and rail lines connected major regions of the north, but did not reach remote areas at all. Port Sudan was opened in 1906, and irrigation programs in the 1920s transformed large sections of central Sudan into farmland. Less money was spent to develop the south, although the area had good potential for agriculture.

Horatio Herbert Kitchener led the Egyptian forces that defeated the Mahdists at Omdurman in 1898 and became the first governor-general of Anglo-Egyptian Sudan.

British missionaries brought the Christian faith to the southern regions of Sudan and helped to create a generation of Westernized African leaders.

European Influence in the South

The Condominium Agreement also put the southern regions of Sudan under British rule. Remote and underdeveloped, the southern provinces had most of their contact with Europeans through Christian missionaries. The missionaries operated schools and health clinics, initially without British support. Graduates of these mission facilities were the first choices to fill civil service posts in the south. In this way, the south's political power base developed from a Christian, English-speaking foundation, while in the north Islam and Arabic prevailed within the bureaucracy.

With the intent of eventually combining southern Sudan with Tanzania, Uganda, and Kenya, Great Britain actively encouraged the southern provinces to identify

Under the Condominium Agreement, the southern provinces were encouraged to identify themselves with Britain's East African colonies. Villages, such as this one near the southern town of Uwayl, were hardly touched by development projects that were organized in the north.

themselves with these British colonies in East Africa. The government barred northern Sudanese from traveling to the south, and it prevented southerners from seeking employment in the more developed north. An announcement in 1930 decreed that southern blacks were to regard themselves as ethnically distinct from the Arabs of the north.

Road to Independence

Amid these internal conflicts, two political parties emerged in the 1940s. The National Unionist party (NUP) favored union with Egypt, while the Umma party wanted independence for Sudan. In 1948 the British established a Sudanese legislative assembly, and in that year's elections, which the NUP boycotted, the Umma gained a majority of seats.

In the meantime, disagreement grew between Britain and Egypt over the future of Sudan. In 1951 Egypt rejected the Condominium Agreement and declared Egypt's King Farouk I to be king of Sudan. After the overthrow of the Egyptian monarchy in 1952, however, Egypt abandoned its claim to Sudan. In 1953 the Egyptians and the British drew up a new treaty, paving the way for Sudanese independence. The NUP participated in the elections held in 1953 and won a clear majority. The NUP's leader, Ismail al-Azhari, formed a colonial government in 1954.

As the British turned more and more control over to the Sudanese, southerners saw signs of domination by the north. The new legislature chose Arabic—formerly forbidden as a language in the south—as the official language of administration throughout Sudan. The former policy of isolating the southern provinces gave way to an openness in the realms of trade and employment, and northerners began to take over key positions in the southern

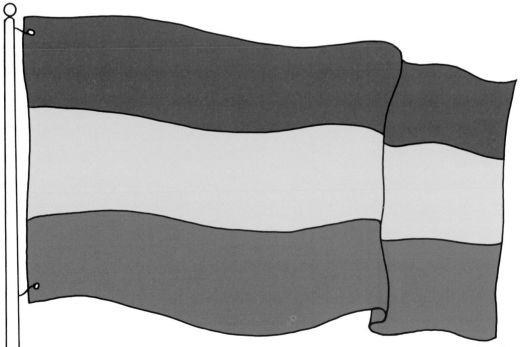

Artwork by Steven Woods

Sudan's flag at independence in 1956 was composed of three horizontal stripes. Blue represented the Nile River, yellow stood for the desert, and green symbolized the nation's vegetation.

After 1956, coalition governments in Sudan found that Western administrative methods did not work in a country with such diverse ethnic groups. Regional and religious ties were strong, and some of the southern groups rebelled because they felt that the north was trying to control them.

Internal conflicts—including the outbreak of civil war in the south—that stagnated the political process encouraged the army to take over the government of Sudan in 1958. A military council governed the country until 1964, when parliamentary rule was restored. Civilian rule lasted until 1969, when a young military officer, Colonel Jaffar Mohammed Nimeiry, assumed power in a second coup d'état. In 1971, after another overthrow was nearly successful, Nimeiry was elected by general vote to a six-year term as president.

The Nimeiry Era

Throughout his term as Sudan's leader, Nimeiry thwarted many coup attempts by

Independent Picture Service

On Sudan's Independence Day, January 1, 1956, the new republic's flag was raised as Prime Minister Ismail al-Azhari and the leader of the opposition party, Muhammed Ahmad Mahjub, look on.

administration. Furthermore, Muslims were no longer barred from trying to gain religious converts in the south.

Independence and Its Aftermath

Although union with Egypt was the main idea in the NUP's political platform, anti-union riots and demonstrations convinced the Azhari government to change its position radically. Azhari publicly announced that he was in favor of Sudanese independence and called for a withdrawal of foreign troops. The Sudanese legislature unanimously passed a declaration of Sudanese independence on December 19, 1955, and the nation formally became a self-governing republic on January 1, 1956.

Courtesy of John Dean, Eliot Elisofon Archives, National Museum of African Art, Smithsonian Institution

General Ibrahim Abboud, commander of the Sudanese army and leader of the 1958 coup d'état, greeted his staff after the military takeover.

33

From 1971 until 1985, Jaffar Nimeiry served as president of Sudan. Civil war in the south and demonstrations in the north plagued his administration, which was overthrown in 1985.

A decade after signing the agreement in Addis Ababa, however, Nimeiry weakened the authority of the south by dividing the region into three parts. He also imposed strict Islamic law throughout the country, a decision that particularly angered the non-Muslim southern population. The establishment of the Sudanese People's Liberation Army (SPLA) soon followed, and civil war in the southern provinces has affected Sudan's stability ever since.

After 16 years of Nimeiry's rule, army officers overthrew the president in April 1985. Escalating civil war in the south, Nimeiry's poor economic management, governmental corruption, and reactions to police repression contributed to the coup's success. More important, however, was the riot triggered by a huge increase in bread prices, which Nimeiry announced only days before the coup.

New Regimes

Shortly after taking power, the coup's leaders announced a program to return to civilian rule within a year. In an orderly election in 1986, the people of Sudan—with the exception of the southerners, who boycotted the election—voted a majority of seats in the legislature to the conservative Umma party. It formed a coalition with the delegates of the Democratic Unionist party, and the coalition selected Sadiq al-Mahdi as prime minister.

The new government faced Sudan's ongoing problems—civil war, famine, and economic decline. The war continued, and towns under the control of the SPLA became scenes of fighting and starvation. Drought in neighboring countries brought many refugees to Sudan, which was unable to feed them. Thousands of people died as troops—both of the government and of the SPLA—prevented relief food from getting to the south. In addition, heavy rains in 1988 caused massive flooding in the

military officers who opposed his rule. He also faced civilian disturbances led by various political and ethnic movements that disagreed with his policies. Frustrated by inflation, food shortages, and other economic hardships, these groups staged numerous public demonstrations. They wanted to expose the regime's inability to provide basic opportunities for Sudan's people. In 1974, faced with labor and student unrest, Nimeiry declared a state of emergency.

Even after disbanding opposition groups and reshuffling his cabinet to reduce its power to overthrow him, Nimeiry faced troubled times. Riots and civil war—costing the lives of 500,000 Sudanese—continued to plague the Nimeiry government. In 1972, at a historic meeting in Addis Ababa, Ethiopia, the Sudanese government agreed to grant regional authority to the southern Sudanese.

In 1986 western Sudan, which lies within the Sahel near the Sahara Desert, faced drought conditions. Sacks of sorghum, a cereal grain, arrived at some villages, but an inadequate transportation network and the civil war prevented relief supplies from reaching other settlements.

35

Sadiq al-Mahdi, great-grandson of the Mahdi who fought for Sudan's independence in the nineteenth century, led a coalition government of the legislature's two largest political parties from 1986 to 1989.

north, leaving many Sudanese homeless and without food.

The government of Sadiq al-Madhi seemed unable to take action to combat these serious problems, and in June 1989, the army overthrew the civilian regime. Led by General Omar Hassan Ahmed al-Bashir, the coup occurred without bloodshed. Al-Bashir, who named himself prime minister, suspended the constitution, detained members of the former cabinet, and censored the press.

The problems of civil war, famine, and too many refugees also confront the new military regime. Al-Bashir has stated that his first priority is to end the war, but he has neglected to submit a plan for the achievement of this goal. The SPLA's reaction to the change in power is still not clear, but Sudan's future depends on the ending of the conflict before the nation's economy and its population are without hope of recovery.

Government

Military regimes have ruled Sudan for 23 of the past 33 years. Following the 1989 military takeover, political parties were

By building shelters and establishing family compounds, Chadian refugees in a camp at Al-Junaynah in western Sudan organize the settlement into a temporary village.

The appearance of airborne sacks of much-needed grain brings people rushing to the drop site.

banned, and the constitution was suspended. At present, a cabinet headed by General al-Bashir runs the country.

Prior to the coup, the main feature of the Sudanese government was an elected legislature. From this body came both the prime minister, who was head of the government, and an executive council, which acted as head of state. For administrative purposes, Sudan is divided into seven regions, each of which contains more than one province.

The Sudanese judicial system has been influenced by both British and Islamic legal codes. In fact, the imposition of *sharia*, or Islamic law, has been a major point of conflict between the north and the south. It remains to be seen whether the new regime will continue to insist on sharia as the law of the land. Sharia generally covers cases of a personal nature, such as disagreements about inheritance, marriage, and guardianship. A British-based code is used in criminal hearings.

Children in a village of western Sudan play soccer inside their compound, which is fenced by entwined stalks of millet (a cereal grain).

3) The People

The 24.5 million inhabitants of Sudan belong to many ethnic groups and are identified by the languages they speak. The most numerous are the Arabic-speakers, including the Juhayna and the Jaali peoples. Other Muslim groups are the Nubians, the Beja, and the Fur. Non-Muslim groups centered around the Nile speak languages that are called Nilotic.

Ethnic Groups

The Arabic-speaking Juhayna have a reputation as a nomadic (seasonally wandering) people, although some members have become more settled in recent times. The Jaali live along the banks of the Nile between Dunqulah and the area north of Khartoum.

Although they speak Arabic as a second language, the Nubians have their own language and, after the Arabs, are the largest group in Sudan. Residents of the Nile River Valley, they inhabit the country's northernmost reaches and maintain strong ethnic loyalties.

The Beja are a largely nomadic group and live in the Red Sea Hills. Although

The face of a young southern Sudanese woman is adorned with the traditional markings of her people.

The Red Sea Hills of eastern Sudan are the home of this Beja woman, whose language links her to ethnic groups in Ethiopia.

Family relationships—especially between young and old—are among the most important aspects of rural life in Sudan.

they have adopted many Arab customs, their language links them to the Cushitic-speakers of the south.

Having settled in the area around the Jebel Marra Mountains long ago, the Fur composed an independent sultanate until they were absorbed by other powers. Mostly farmers, the Fur have ethnic ties to groups in neighboring Chad.

Most of the non-Muslims to the south are classified as part of the Nilotic ethnic group of black Africans. Those who belong to the largest Nilotic group are cattle raisers living near the Bahr al-Jebel River and its tributaries. Subgroups include the Dinka, Nuer, and Shilluk.

North-South Relations

In 1955, a year before the independence of Sudan, southerners began to voice concern about changes in government policy. The southerners objected to Arabic being made the official language of Sudan and to the replacement of traditional ethnic leaders by northerners. These moves were seen as part of the government's "Arabization" campaign. Bloodshed and armed clashes occurred after southern Sudanese soldiers mutinied against their northern officers. For a time government troops took control of the south.

The campaign of Arabization continued after independence and in the 1960s triggered further conflict in the south. Since then, Sudan has been in a state of civil war, between government forces and troops of the SPLA. The SPLA wants to establish southern Sudan as a self-ruling region, allied with—but not controlled by—the central government.

Education

Progress in education has been slow since independence. The national literacy rate in the 1980s was low—only 20 percent—and

Courtesy of Kay Chernush/Agency for International Development

In a common pose, a Sudanese woman carries her goods on her head and her child in a cloth that hangs around her neck.

In spite of the conflict between government troops and the Sudanese People's Liberation Army (SPLA), a monument in Khartoum commemorates the unity of Sudan's many ethnic groups.

Courtesy of Kenneth J. Perkins

40

Palm trees line the entrance to the main library of Khartoum University, which was called Gordon College in colonial times.

women and girls made up most of the illiterate population. The lack of adequate facilities and school materials and too few teachers have contributed to the low level of educational achievement. In addition, more schools exist in urban areas than in the country. Since most Sudanese live in rural areas, they receive limited schooling.

Sudan's inadequate educational system is most evident in southern, largely non-Arabic regions. Only about 14 percent of all the nation's primary schools are located in the south, where about 25 percent of the Sudanese population lives. The area also has only 7 percent of the total number of secondary schools in Sudan.

Inadequate educational facilities at the primary-school level have hampered Sudan's ability to educate its young people. The United Nations set up this classroom in a rural area of eastern Sudan.

Photo by Jenny Matthews

Children at a school in Labadu, western Sudan, learn Arabic, mathematics, religion, and science. Here, they are reciting verses from the Koran, the Islamic book of sacred writings.

In the 1980s, 48 percent of Sudanese children were enrolled in primary and secondary schools. Students attend six years of schooling at the primary level and three years of secondary classes. Most of the institutions of higher learning are in the north, although by 1980 universities had opened in Juba and El Gezira.

Religion

Islam is Sudan's dominant religion and has supporters among almost all the ethnic groups in the country. Muslims, most of whom speak Arabic, make up about 75 percent of the total Sudanese population. Approximately 95 percent of the northern provinces consist of Arabic-speaking Muslims. Non-Muslims—who subscribe to traditional African or to Christian beliefs —mostly inhabit southern Sudan and constitute no more than 10 percent of the nation's population.

Sudanese Muslims are of the Sunni—or traditional—sect, which features strong Islamic brotherhoods. These religious orders are influential in many African nations and make demands—sometimes including political support—on their followers. In Sudan the Qadiriya is the largest order, but it is also the least organized. The Khatmiya gets most of its support from northeastern Sudan. A strong, centralized order, the Khatmiya is headed by the members of one family and has wielded political power since the late nineteenth century.

Faithful Muslims (followers of Islam) pray five times each day.

An often-repeated Islamic prayer — indeed it is a basic element of Muslim belief — is that there is no God but Allah and that Muhammad is his prophet.

When Sudanese Muslims pray, they face east toward the holy city of Mecca in Saudi Arabia, where Muhammad was born.

43

People whose ancestors originated in southern Sudan often support traditional African religious beliefs. Nilotic communities, for example, believe in a supreme god, the power of nature, and the importance of ancestors. Nevertheless, rituals vary from group to group. The roughly 5 percent of southerners who are Christian form the smallest religious minority in Sudan.

Language and the Arts

Sudan's languages—estimated to number about 100—are an example of the country's ethnic diversity. More than half of the population speak Arabic, which is the official language of Sudan. Used as a first or second language by almost every group in Sudan, Arabic is the language used in schools.

Sudanese literature—including poetry, short stories, and novels—is well known throughout Arab countries. Tayeb Salih is Sudan's most popular writer, and two of

Independent Picture Service

Muezzins (criers) call Muslims to daily prayer from the tall tower, or minaret, of this mosque in the capital city of Khartoum.

Courtesy of Kenneth J. Perkins

In addition to mosques of traditional design, Muslims have built modern structures, such as the Mosque of the Two Niles at Omdurman.

Sudan's silversmiths use their ancient skill to make ornate trays and flasks.

A Sudanese leatherworker cuts out a pair of shoes from a locally produced hide.

An art student in northern Sudan produced this sculpture of a mother and child.

At a market in Omdurman—a city noted for its wealth of handcrafted goods—a goldsmith works on another decorative article.

his novels—*The Wedding of Zein* and *Season of Migration to the North*—have been translated into English.

The silversmiths, ivory-carvers, and leatherworkers of Omdurman are famous, and the southern Sudanese are known for their carved wooden figures. In the eastern and western deserts of Sudan, craftspeople concentrate on making swords and spears.

A young boy in western Sudan separates the fruit of the watermelon from the seeds, which are used to make oil.

Food and Clothing

In times when food is readily available, a common meal in Sudan may feature *ful,* which consists of broad beans cooked in oil. Many Sudanese make pancakes from millet flour, which they eat with highly seasoned soups and stews. Cooks make the stews from herbs and vegetables, such as onions and tomatoes, to which they sometimes add eggs and meat. The nomads of the northern deserts live mainly on dairy products and meat from camels, while the southern Sudanese make their soups with vegetables, including cassavas (starchy roots) or sweet potatoes.

In Sudan's cities, people usually wear Western clothing, although traditional dress is also seen. Islam dictates that women wear an outer garment that covers their head and reaches to their feet. Men may wear a long robe, called a *jallabiyah,* along with either a small cap or a turban. In northern rural areas, however, especially where the daytime temperatures may be very hot, people do not wear much clothing.

To make peanut sauces, the peanuts must be shelled and roasted. The nuts are ground into a paste, usually by rolling them against a hard rock with a heavy tool.

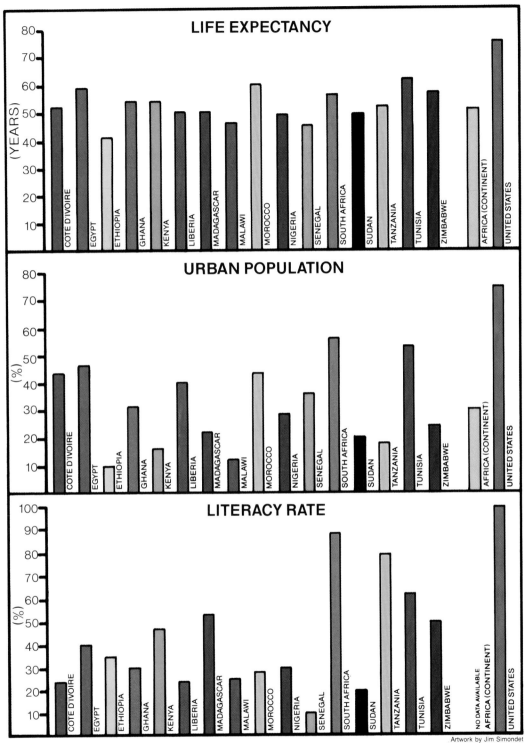

LIFE EXPECTANCY

(YEARS)

COTE D'IVOIRE · EGYPT · ETHIOPIA · GHANA · KENYA · LIBERIA · MADAGASCAR · MALAWI · MOROCCO · NIGERIA · SENEGAL · SOUTH AFRICA · SUDAN · TANZANIA · TUNISIA · ZIMBABWE · AFRICA (CONTINENT) · UNITED STATES

URBAN POPULATION

(%)

COTE D'IVOIRE · EGYPT · ETHIOPIA · GHANA · KENYA · LIBERIA · MADAGASCAR · MALAWI · MOROCCO · NIGERIA · SENEGAL · SOUTH AFRICA · SUDAN · TANZANIA · TUNISIA · ZIMBABWE · AFRICA (CONTINENT) · UNITED STATES

LITERACY RATE

(%)

COTE D'IVOIRE · EGYPT · ETHIOPIA · GHANA · KENYA · LIBERIA · MADAGASCAR · MALAWI · MOROCCO · NIGERIA · SENEGAL · SOUTH AFRICA · SUDAN · TANZANIA · TUNISIA · ZIMBABWE · NO DATA AVAILABLE AFRICA (CONTINENT) · UNITED STATES

Artwork by Jim Simondet

The three factors depicted in this graph suggest differences in the quality of life among 16 African nations. Averages for the United States and the entire continent of Africa are included for comparison. (Data from "1987 World Population Data Sheet" and *PC-Globe*.)

Drought, and the consequent outbreak of famine in the 1980s, brought many refugees to Sudan from neighboring Chad, Uganda, and Ethiopia. As a result, severe pressures have been put on Sudan's food resources. Here, the contents of sacks of grain are distributed to the inhabitants of a refugee camp to supplement their daily diets.

Health

Poor diet and environmental conditions cause far-reaching health problems in Sudan. In cooperation with international agencies, such as the World Health Organization (WHO), the Sudanese government has begun eliminating smallpox and other diseases. Malaria, tuberculosis, and dysentery continue to afflict Sudan's low-income groups, however. Less than half of all Sudanese have access to safe drinking water, a situation that further complicates health care.

Life expectancy in Sudan is 49 years, and the infant mortality rate is 113 for every 1,000 live births. Though far worse than Western figures, both statistics are about average for African countries.

Malnutrition is a major problem in Sudan. In the rural south, for example, poverty is widespread, and malnutrition makes children more vulnerable to diseases. It is estimated that one-fourth of the total Sudanese population has suffered from malnutrition in the 1980s. The thousands of deaths in eastern and southern Sudan during the outbreak of famine in the 1980s clearly show the health threat facing both rural Sudanese and large refugee populations.

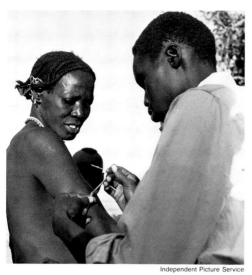

Independent Picture Service

A traveling health-care professional administers a smallpox vaccination to a woman in southern Sudan.

Courtesy of M. Gaieb/FAO

Safe drinking water is an essential part of limiting disease in Sudan. Here, women collect fresh water from a recently built village supply point.

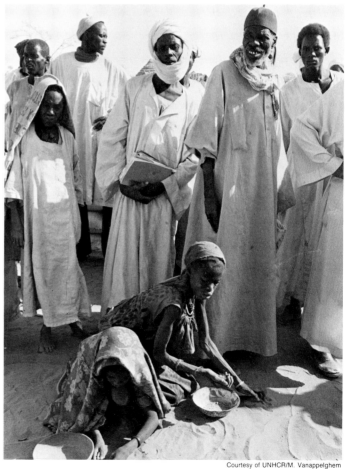

In areas where malnutrition is a severe health problem, even the scattered grains collected by children become important.

Courtesy of UNHCR/M. Vanappelghem

Photo by Jenny Matthews

Market day in Labadu brings buyers and sellers from miles around the small town in western Sudan.

4) The Economy

Sudan's economy is beset by many problems, which make it difficult for the country to achieve financial security and to reach long-range goals of modernization. Agriculture is the focus of the Sudanese economy. The quality of the harvest—along with world prices for the nation's cash-producing crops—determines the health of the economy in a given year.

Development of the economy at all levels is slow because of an inadequate transportation network and because of the loss of

experienced workers to high-paying jobs in other Arab countries. Financial instability—which has caused other nations to stop lending money to Sudan in recent times—forced the government to cut back on development projects in the late 1980s.

Agriculture

Sudan is an agricultural society, and 80 percent of its people are engaged in farming and livestock raising. Agriculture

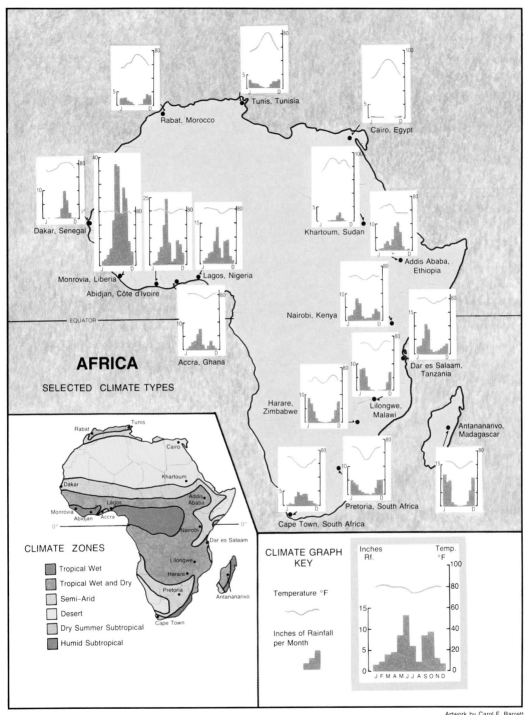

AFRICA

SELECTED CLIMATE TYPES

Rabat, Morocco

Tunis, Tunisia

Cairo, Egypt

Dakar, Senegal

Khartoum, Sudan

Addis Ababa, Ethiopia

Monrovia, Liberia

Abidjan, Côte d'Ivoire

Lagos, Nigeria

Nairobi, Kenya

Accra, Ghana

Dar es Salaam, Tanzania

Harare, Zimbabwe

Lilongwe, Malawi

Antananarivo, Madagascar

Pretoria, South Africa

Cape Town, South Africa

EQUATOR

CLIMATE ZONES

Tropical Wet

Tropical Wet and Dry

Semi-Arid

Desert

Dry Summer Subtropical

Humid Subtropical

Rabat

Tunis

Cairo

Dakar

Khartoum

Addis Ababa

Lagos

Monrovia

Abidjan

Accra

Nairobi

Dar es Salaam

Lilongwe

Harare

Pretoria

Antananarivo

Cape Town

0°

0°

CLIMATE GRAPH KEY

Temperature °F

Inches of Rainfall per Month

Inches Rf.

Temp. °F

100

80

60

40

20

0

15

10

5

0

J F M A M J J A S O N D

Artwork by Carol F. Barrett

These climate graphs show the monthly change in the average rainfall received and in the average temperature from January to December for the capital cities of 16 African nations. Khartoum, Sudan, with about six inches of annual rainfall, has a decidedly dry climate. Notice that no month receives more than three inches of rain, and some months get none at all. The wetter summer months moderate the capital's generally high temperatures. (Data from *World-Climates* by Willy Rudloff, Stuttgart, 1981.)

51

Traditional farming methods are still used in much of Sudan.

Using seeds and water provided by the United Nations, a farmer produces crops despite the drought in the Red Sea Hills.

accounts for 95 percent of Sudan's total export trade and employs most of the labor force. It is estimated that one-third of the land suitable for crops is used for agriculture. In the central part of the country along the Nile, farm machinery helps to produce food for export. Subsistence farmers—those who raise crops only to feed their families—rely on traditional methods of working the soil.

CROPS

The chief crops, which account for 40 percent of the nation's output, are cotton, oilseeds, and cereals. Sudan also supplies four-fifths of the world's gum arabic, which is obtained from acacia trees. The gum is used to manufacture adhesives, candies, and drugs.

Covering 1.1 million acres, a government-owned farm in the fertile El Gezira region is one of the largest nationalized projects in the world. The main cash crop of the farming scheme is cotton, but millet, sorghum, and rice are also grown for local consumption. In the 1980s wheat production increased because of the introduction of a strong variety of the grain. Peanuts grow well in El Gezira's heavy clay soil. Better roads have attracted more farmers to the region.

Women clean and sort gum arabic—a substance used in candies and medicines—at a warehouse in Port Sudan.

Using mallets, farmers begin the long process of threshing their grain.

Workers collect the solidified, walnut-sized chunks of gum that ooze from acacia trees. Sudan supplies most of the world's gum arabic, which comes from the species *Acacia arabica* found throughout northern Africa.

To expand the range of their agricultural products, Sudanese farmers have increased their acreages of sugarcane.

53

Photo by Jenny Matthews

In the more arid areas of Sudan, farmers raise a variety of animals—some of which, like goats, are tougher than others—to guard against times when sources of water and pastureland have been exhausted.

Sudanese farmers use a cultivation system called *harig*, under which they let native grasses (harig) spread until the grasses form a dense mat over the land. Then, after the early rains have nourished weed seeds under the mat, a dry spell allows farmers to burn off all the grass and weeds. This process leaves the land refertilized and ready for planting.

LIVESTOCK

Livestock raising supports 40 percent of the Sudanese population. Sudanese herders tend about 50 million animals—chiefly cattle, sheep, goats, and camels—mostly in a traditional rural setting. Herds graze throughout the countryside, except in the extremely dry areas of the north and in the southern regions, where disease-carrying tsetse flies cause illness and death among livestock.

Drought

Parts of Sudan are located in the Sahel, a region along the edge of the Sahara Desert. Drought has hit this area frequently since the mid-1960s. In major irrigated areas of the eastern and central regions of Sudan, low rainfall has reduced crop production. The dry spell mostly has affected subsistence farmers and nomadic populations. These peoples have lost their crops and livestock and have moved to the southern portions of drought-stricken provinces and to the banks of the Nile River.

The famine crisis that emerged in Sudan during the 1980s was far greater than any other food shortage in the country's history. The United Nations estimated that the drought severely affected a total of 4.5 million people in Darfur, Kordofan, and Red Sea provinces. This crisis, as well as

An Ethiopian mother mourns the death of her child in a refugee camp located in eastern Sudan.

the civil war, resulted in substantial food shortages between 1980 and 1989.

The arrival of famine victims from the dry and war-torn nations of Ethiopia, Chad, and Uganda has further complicated Sudan's food crisis. These new arrivals gather in refugee camps located along Sudan's western, eastern, and southern borders. Furthermore, as civil war in southern Sudan continues, mass starvation has resulted because traditional food-producing activities have become too dangerous to practice in areas affected by war. The conflict also prevents food from entering the region.

Photo by Jean Pieri

Photo by Jenny Matthews

As a consequence of severe drought, these children are able to walk through a dried-up riverbed in search of plants for food and wood for fuel.

55

Although Sudan's forests are dwindling, tractors sometimes clear land for agricultural use.

Forestry and Fishing

Large areas of Sudan's forests have been cleared for agricultural use. This process has contributed to the expansion of the desert in semi-arid regions that lie between true desert and wooded areas. Nevertheless, southern Sudan still has extensive forested lands, where hardwoods thrive. One of the main forest products is mahogany timber, which is used in furniture making. The government has authorized the development of plantations for teak and oak in an effort to replenish the dwindling forests. Eucalyptus trees also have been planted in irrigated agricultural areas to protect the soil from erosion and to supply wood as fuel to local residents.

Sudan's fishing industry centers on the Nile River system. Fishing along the coast of the Red Sea and in artificial inland lakes also has been developed. Although Sudan has great potential for a thriving fish industry, most catches have fallen below anticipated levels. Moreover, rather than becoming sources of export income, fish hauls have been needed locally as foodstuffs.

In areas of scrub vegetation, trees provide shelter, fuel, and a place to hang storage bales.

A fisherman throws out his net at the Jebel Aulia Dam, a water-storage facility near Khartoum.

Mill laborers operate machines that separate seeds from cotton grown at El Gezira.

Workers sort batteries at an assembly plant in northern Sudan.

Mining and Industry

Mining contributes little to the national economy, but Sudan is reputed to have substantial mineral deposits. Chromium, mica (a thin, transparent metal), and gypsum (a mineral used in making plaster) form the core of Sudan's current mining industry. Chromium is produced largely in the Ingessana Hills of Blue Nile province. Mica exists in Northern province, and gypsum is found along the coast of the Red Sea. Substantial finds of petroleum have been uncovered in the Upper Nile region, but civil war in the south has prevented development of this resource.

Sudan's manufacturing sector focuses on light industries that use raw materials from the nation's agricultural output. Foodstuffs and textiles account for much of the total of manufactured products. Paper mills and sugar refineries have been built, and several factories turn out products such as beverages and shoes. This part of the economy is hampered by the absence of a strong transportation network and by the lack of cheap and efficient energy sources.

Courtesy of Agency for International Development

With deft movements, an expert brickmaker piles mud into a mold, which will be laid out to dry in the sun.

Energy

Wood and charcoal are the principal energy sources in Sudanese homes, and hydropower and imported oil fill the needs of

For most rural Sudanese, wood is the principal source of fuel and is gathered daily.

Photo by Jenny Matthews

59

The Roseires Dam on the Blue Nile is a major source of hydroelectric power in the north. Its stored water is also being used to irrigate thousands of acres of potential farmland.

Courtesy of Agency for International Development

industry. As Sudan's population has increased, the pressure on natural fuel sources, such as wood, also has grown. Expansion of the desert and shortages of fuel have resulted from the unregulated harvesting of Sudan's forests.

The Blue Nile is dammed at several places, including Sennar, to generate hydroelectricity, although originally the dams were to provide water for irrigation. Hydropower plants, such as the Roseires Dam, supply electricity to urban centers in the north. Nevertheless, four-fifths of the nation's energy needs are met by importing costly foreign oil. A few refineries operate in Sudan. They are able to support the fuel needs of thermal energy plants, which burn refined petroleum products.

Courtesy of Kenneth J. Perkins

Completed in 1937, the Jebel Aulia Dam holds back the floodwaters of the Nile, which arrive between July and October.

Transportation

Two railways operate in Sudan. The British built the Sudan Railway in the late nineteenth century, linking central Sudan to Egypt and the Mediterranean Sea. The El Gezira Light Railway was constructed to connect Khartoum with the fertile cotton-growing regions of central Sudan. Although they need renovation, Sudan's 8,000 miles of track are able to transport heavy freight and much agricultural produce.

Most roads in Sudan are unpaved. All-weather routes connect Port Sudan to Khartoum, but most of the rest are little more than earthen tracks that are passable only in fair weather. Small amounts of freight—especially shipments that are needed quickly—travel by road in the dry season.

Despite its many cataracts—which seriously inhibit navigation—the Nile River is a major inland transportation route for Sudan. Two reaches, or stretches of navigable waterway, exist. The reach in southern Sudan goes from Kusti to Juba, and the other reach extends between Kuraymah and Dunqulah. Equipment breakdowns, however, slow travel on both stretches of the waterway.

Sudan's railway system, originally built by the British, is among the longest in Africa. Trains are slow, however, and carry heavy goods, farm products, and people to destinations throughout northern Sudan.

Dhows are the chief means of transportation on navigable stretches of the Nile.

Photo by Jenny Matthews

Field-workers in western Sudan take water to the farm site that lies an hour's walk from their village.

Photo by Jenny Matthews

Camels are still a popular – and practical – form of travel in dry regions because the animals can go without water for many days.

The Future

Located in a region that once was influenced by the cultures of ancient Egypt and Nubia, Sudan has had periods of prosperity. Modern Sudan, however, struggles to survive. Its entire foreign debt is equal to the total amount of goods produced by the nation each year. Its southern provinces are the scene of constant conflict. Famine and drought have affected the livelihoods, migration patterns, and health standards of countless Sudanese.

Although the new regime of General al-Bashir faces grave challenges, Sudanese cultural traditions are strong and vital. And, as a nation with connections to both the African and Arab worlds, Sudan may have an important international role to play. These strengths may help the nation to mend its civil conflicts and to deal with the problems of hunger and economic strife.

Photo by Jenny Matthews

One of Sudan's cultural strengths is the central importance of family life. In rural areas, some families live in compounds —fenced areas containing several dwellings where members of one family reside together. All relatives, from children to grandparents, work to furnish the food and marketable goods that support the family. Because Muslim laws allow a man to have more than one wife—if he treats them all the same—many families are quite large.

Photo by Jenny Matthews

During recent periods of drought, the Sudanese have used other sources of food—such as this wild plant called *mukheit*—as part of their diets.

63

Index